Invest in the Wall Street Stock Exchange (United States) (Updated era Biden and Vaccine) 2020 2021:

Money-making operation for the coronavirus pandemic

Antonio Robinhood

Index
The best stock market in the world: diversity and volume 5
My operation to make money from the pandemic 6
Positions Closed During the Pandemic 9
Trading to make money on the US stock market 11
Favourite actions: the best you can find! 15
Update: The J. Biden Era and the Pfizer Vaccine 21
Gift: 20 euros for you and me 24
Farewell 26

"Wall Street is the only place that people ride to in a Rolls Royce to get advice from those who take the subway". Warren Buffett.

The best stock market in the world: diversity and volume

In the U.S. the options are many and my portfolio is also diverse.

It is the best stock exchange in the world because it is where there is more capital, all the entrepreneurs and investors want to have their piece of the pie. It can boast of hosting leading companies in the world, capable of making you money non-stop and effortlessly.

In this book, similar to the previous one in this same series (*Investing in the Stock Market with Intelligence),* although taking into account the particularities, I am going to show you what my operations are during the pandemic in the Yankee stock market. The historical evolution of this stock market makes it very attractive. If you compare it with the Spanish one, you will see that the United States crises are history and that, despite living through great falls, it has always managed to recover and overcome itself until now. The Spanish stock market, on the other hand, has not yet returned to the levels of the beginning of the century.

Compare graphs of the indices of both exchanges to see this fact. It is also important for you to know that in the American stock market you can find stocks that have always been paying more dividends for more than fifty years. You can find the list by searching for Dividend Kings, also the ones that have been accumulating for twenty-five years, the Dividend Queens.

My operation to make money from the pandemic

It was in June (of 2020) when I started my investments. As I anticipated, the number of companies you can find is immense. I'm going to start by showing you my portfolio, first the positions I still have open, and then the ones I've already closed (and withdrawn profits).

Acciones

Producto ▲

C V ⋮	AT&T	A
C V ⋮	American Express Company	C
C V ⋮	Aurora Cannabis	D
C V ⋮	Bank of America Corp	C
C V ⋮	Barrick Gold Corp	B
C V ⋮	Brookfield Asset Management	C
C V ⋮	Canopy Growth Corp	D
C V ⋮	Carnival Corp	D
C V ⋮	Coca-Cola Company	A
C V ⋮	Genius Brands International	D
C V ⋮	Gilead Sciences	A
C V ⋮	Intel Corp	B
C V ⋮	Johnson & Johnson	A
C V ⋮	MTBC	D
C V ⋮	Maxeon Solar Technologies ...	D
C V ⋮	PNC Financial Services Group	C

C V : Pfizer	A
C V : Realty Income Corp	C
C V : STORE Capital Corp	C
C V : Simon Property Group	D
C V : Starbucks Corp	B
C V : SunPower Corp	D
C V : Virgin Galactic Holdings	D
C V : Walt Disney Company (The)	B
C V : Workhorse Group	D

These are the ones I have, as you see, there is almost everything. The letter indicates the "quality" of the stock according to its history, A is the best.

I have avoided saying exactly how much money I have in each stock for security reasons, but I do want to explain what percentage of my portfolio each sector, or type of stock, represents.

The sectors in which I have more money are: pharmaceutical, financial, *real estate,* telecoms, services (entertainment, tourism, marijuana...) and solar energy. Then we have three companies that are difficult to group with the rest. I believe that Intel needs no introduction to anyone, its competition with AMD and some delays in projects have made its quotation fall and, since I opened my position, I have been increasing it. They say that their management is not the best, but the truth is that they have a huge business and will benefit from the pandemic. And, best of all, even if it doesn't go up in price, I don't care: it pays dividends. Virgin Galactic is less well known, it's a company that sells trips to the moon, in short. It's a growth stock, very speculative, and it has already gone up in price a lot since I opened my position and I have already sold part of the shares I had, earning money. The third stock that deserves individual treatment is Workhorse, a company that manufactures electronic trucks and which has also already allowed me to withdraw profits, without having yet disposed of all my shares (I don't have many left, I don't invest much in these speculative stocks).

I also have quite speculative (growth) actions in the marijuana sector: Aurora Cannabis and Canopy Growth. Both have grown in a beastly way with the victory of Joe Biden.

More than 70% of my portfolio is in shares of very strong, established companies that distribute dividends. The rest is speculation that allows me to withdraw money almost every month.

I never get too attached to a share, although I like it, if it is worth more than I think it is, I sell it. I will have the opportunity to buy it back when the market realizes it and corrects (that's what they call dropping or lowering the price).

Positions Closed During the Pandemic

Below, I show you the five companies I no longer have positions in. With the first three I made very good profits, with the other two (TripAdvisor and Uber Technologies) I decided to sell, although without big profits, to invest in safer options.

Acciones

Producto	
C V : First Solar	C
C V : McDonald's Corp	A
C V : NIO	D
C V : TripAdvisor	C
C V : Uber Technologies	C

These are the shares that I have bought but no longer have any (closed positions). Only one of them is a dividend stock, McDonald's, the others are growth stocks.

First Solar is the one that has given me the most money so far, I started with a position that occupied about 25% of the American portfolio and about 17% of my total portfolio (including the shares in Spain). I bought the shares at $50 and sold them from $60 to $93. I don't know if they're still going up, but I can't complain about the profit they've given me.

I still have positions in solar, SunPower has gone up over 80% since I bought, I've already sold half my position, and I have an automatic order to sell what's left as soon as I hit $21 per share (I bought at $9). Update: With Biden's victory, SunPower's price per share reached $21 and I closed my position.

TripAdvisor and Uber I bought them to speculate. Uber seems to me that he has more future, if he manages to stay the market of the automated transport (cars without drivers), his action will reach the sky. However, it's a very competitive struggle and I've preferred to withdraw profits and put the money into more stable businesses (Uber still doesn't make profits, he invests everything to get greater market shares).

TripAdvisor I bought it because I thought it was a bargain, but after a few weeks with a lot of volatility and no clear growth (in view of the fact that the pandemic doesn't seem to be ending), I decided to sell for a little more than it cost and put the money into dividend shares.

In renewable energies, I continue to have investments with Brookfield Asset Management: a Canadian multinational that is dedicated to asset management and distributes dividends. And in Maxeon Solar Technologies, a strategic spin-off from SunPower. Both, at less than $35 for the former and less than $20 for the latter, are excellent investments. Even at higher prices, $45 or $50 for the former and up to $40 for the latter are still opportunities to make money during the pandemic.

Trading to make money on the US stock market

It is important that, when you buy shares that distribute dividends and are from the U.S. stock market, check if your broker has an agreement with your country to reduce double taxation. This way you won't have to pay as much tax to both countries to collect your dividends. This is the famous Form W8, if it is applicable you will not need to do anything: you will pay "only" 15% to each country, otherwise you will pay 30% to the USA and, if you live in Spain, 20% (in each country there is a different tax rate). There is no way to make this agreement as an individual, it has to be the broker who has it. In Degiro you can see it in the product information section, to the right of the graph:

The logic behind my investments is the same as in the Spanish case: the crisis will pass. Although this time we have many more opportunities. Legendary companies such as Disney and Coca-Cola are very safe investments and, because of the confinement, we were able to find them at very profitable prices. Solar and pharmaceutical companies are also leaders in their markets.

The pandemic accelerates digitalization, which will give money to the companies that manufacture the computer parts (Intel) and offer the connection services (AT&T and Telefonica). The sedentary life and the use of the mask, besides the coronavirus, will give enormous benefits to the pharmaceutical companies: Gilead Science, Pfizer, Johnson & Johnson... When the coronavirus is controlled, tourism will return (Carnival, NH, Meliá...). When the economy grows, the banks will give credits, they will make money and the price of their shares will rise (PNC, Santander, Bank of America...). If confidence in the economy fails, gold will rise in price (Barrick Gold...).

The energy transition is a fact and the commitment to renewable energies is very secure, the doubt is, in a competitive scenario, which companies will keep the cake.

Starbucks, McDonald's and Coca-Cola, although they have suffered from the downturn in the economy, have not done so as much as their competitors: small businesses are going bankrupt and giving larger ones a greater market share.

Realty Income, STORE Capital and Simon Property Group allow me to invest in real estate without having to make the related arrangements. Like most of the stock market, its price fell due to the effect of the lockouts, giving a great opportunity for purchase. They are companies that pay dividends consistently and, although they may take time to recover, you can keep them in your portfolio for a lifetime and you won't regret it.

A great advantage of the American stock market is that you can invest in the economy of other countries. In my operation there are shares of companies from Germany, Canada and China. The German company is First Solar. NIO is the Chinese one, an electric car company, the Chinese government owns 30%. Its price has risen spectacularly (it has already exceeded 40).

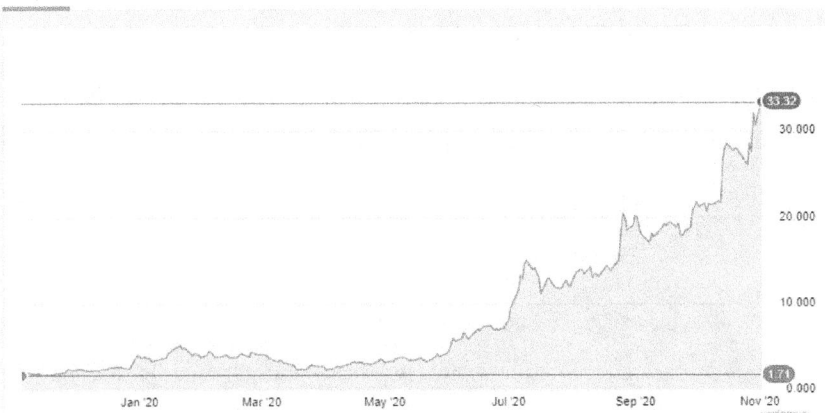

There are too many actions to mention all of them without getting bored. If you are particularly interested in any of them, I encourage you to investigate them and draw your own conclusions. What I want to demonstrate is that it is not only possible to make money from the stock market during the pandemic, it is even easy, if you invest on a logical basis and following a method to periodically withdraw profits without giving up a large part of the portfolio in dividend shares that give you those wonderful passive incomes.

There are too many actions to mention all of them without getting bored. If you are particularly interested in any of them, I encourage you to investigate them and draw your own conclusions. What I want to demonstrate is that it is not only possible to make money from the stock market during the pandemic, it is even easy, if you invest on a logical basis and following a method to periodically withdraw profits without giving up a large part of the portfolio in dividend shares that give you those wonderful passive incomes.

Operating if you like to, is much riskier than simply investing in dividend shares. Trying never to sell, of course. Buy to hold is the safest strategy for stable and growing returns. But, realistically, dividends in the US stock market are lower than in the Spanish one (although safer and less time consuming) and living off them requires many millions. In other words, obtaining financial freedom only with dividends is something reserved for those who already have so much money that they are probably already free. On the other hand, operating, buying and selling, like surfing through the cycles of finance, allows you to earn much, much money, in a short time.

The relationship between profitability and risk is always the same: that which can give you more money is the most dangerous. That's why trading can also make you angry, so that you are bitter, use only money that you are willing to lose.

Favourite actions: the best you can find!

I'm going to share with you the list of actions that I have in the list of favorites in Degiro, they are options that I find very interesting, especially if, for some situation, they lower their prices.

Producto ▲	
★ [C] [V] ⋮ 3M	[A]
★ [C] [V] ⋮ ABM Industries	[C]
★ [C] [V] ⋮ AIRBUS	[C]
★ [C] [V] ⋮ AIRBUS GROUP, S.E.	[C]
★ [C] [V] ⋮ ALIBABA GROUP HO…	[A]
★ [C] [V] ⋮ AbbVie	[A]
★ [C] [V] ⋮ Advanced Micro Devic…	[C]
★ [C] [V] ⋮ Alphabet	[A]
★ [C] [V] ⋮ Altria Group Inc.	[A]
★ [C] [V] ⋮ Amazon.com Inc.	[A]
★ [C] [V] ⋮ America Movil Sa	[B]
★ [C] [V] ⋮ American States Wate…	[B]
★ [C] [V] ⋮ Amgen Inc.	[A]
★ [C] [V] ⋮ Amundi Index MSCI …	[H]
★ [C] [V] ⋮ Apple Inc	[B]

★	C V	⋮	Automatic Data Proce...	B
★	C V	⋮	BROADCOM INC. - C...	C
★	C V	⋮	Berkshire Hathaway B	A
★	C V	⋮	Boeing	D
★	C V	⋮	CROWDSTRIKE HOL...	D
★	C V	⋮	California Water Servi...	B
★	C V	⋮	Cincinnati Financial C...	C
★	C V	⋮	Cisco Systems	B
★	C V	⋮	Commerce Bancshares	B
★	C V	⋮	Constellation Brands	C

Producto	
★ C V ⋮ DOWDUPONT INC. C...	C
★ C V ⋮ Darden Restaurants	D
★ C V ⋮ Delta Air Lines Inc	C
★ C V ⋮ Dover Corp	B
★ C V ⋮ Ebay Inc	A
★ C V ⋮ Emerson Electric	C
★ C V ⋮ Etsy	C
★ C V ⋮ ExxonMobil Corp	B
★ C V ⋮ FARMERS & MERCH...	D
★ C V ⋮ FASTLY INC. CLASS ...	D
★ C V ⋮ Facebook	B
★ C V ⋮ FedEx Corp	C
★ C V ⋮ Federal Realty Invest...	C
★ C V ⋮ Ferrari	A
★ C V ⋮ Five Below	C
★ C V ⋮ Fortinet Inc	C

★ C V ⋮	GROWGENERATION...	D
★ C V ⋮	General Mills	A
★ C V ⋮	HB Fuller Co	B
★ C V ⋮	HSBC Holdings Plc	A
★ C V ⋮	Home Depot	B
★ C V ⋮	Hormel Foods Corp	A
★ C V ⋮	IBM	A
★ C V ⋮	ING Groep	C
★ C V ⋮	International Business...	C

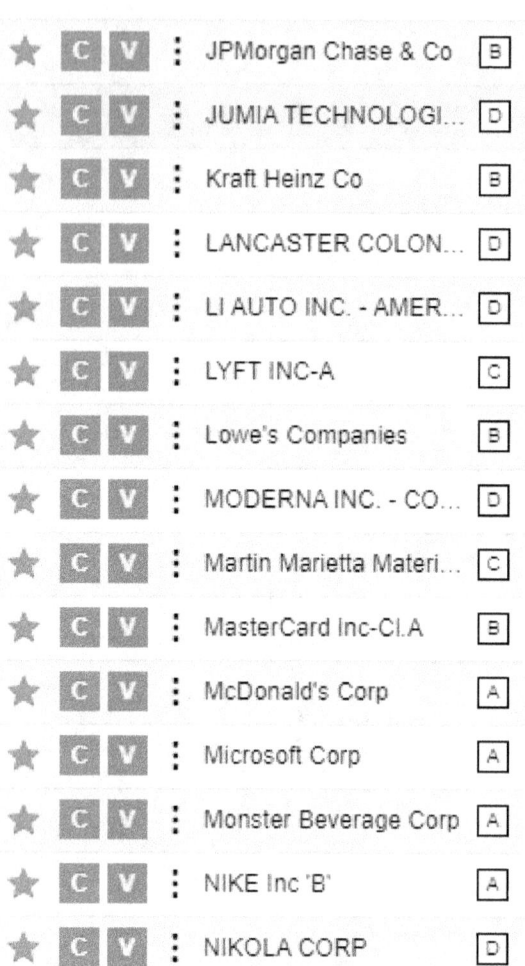

★	C V	⋮	NORTHWEST NATU…	C
★	C V	⋮	NVIDIA CORPORATI…	C
★	C V	⋮	Netflix Inc	C
★	C V	⋮	NextEra Energy Inc	A
★	C V	⋮	Nordson Corp	B
★	C V	⋮	ONEOK Inc	D
★	C V	⋮	Ollie's Bargain Outlet …	C
★	C V	⋮	PEPSICO INC	A
★	C V	⋮	Parker-Hannifin	C

- ★ C V ⋮ PayPal Holdings Inc — B
- ★ C V ⋮ Performance Food Gr... — D
- ★ C V ⋮ Plug Power Inc. — D
- ★ C V ⋮ Porsche Automobil Ho... — B
- ★ C V ⋮ Procter & Gamble — A
- ★ C V ⋮ Qualcomm — B
- ★ C V ⋮ Realty Income — C
- ★ C V ⋮ Restaurant Brands Int... — D
- ★ C V ⋮ Royal Caribbean Crui... — D
- ★ C V ⋮ SJW Group — B
- ★ C V ⋮ SOCIAL CAPITAL HE... — D
- ★ C V ⋮ SONY CORPORATIO... — A
- ★ C V ⋮ SP Plus Corporation — C
- ★ C V ⋮ SPDR S&P US Divide... — H
- ★ C V ⋮ SSgA SPDR Barclays ... — F
- ★ C V ⋮ SSgA SPDR Barclays ... — F

★	C V ⋮	STABLE ROAD ACQ...	D
★	C V ⋮	STONECO LTD-A	D
★	C V ⋮	STORE Capital	C
★	C V ⋮	Shopify	C
★	C V ⋮	Skyworks Solutions	C
★	C V ⋮	Square	C
★	C V ⋮	Stanley Black & Deck...	C
★	C V ⋮	Stepan Co.	B
★	C V ⋮	Sysco Corp	C
★	C V ⋮	TAPESTRY INC	D

★	C V	⋮	TELADOC HEALTH I...	D
★	C V	⋮	Target Corp	B
★	C V	⋮	Tesla	D
★	C V	⋮	Texas Instruments	B
★	C V	⋮	Tootsie Roll Industries	B
★	C V	⋮	TripAdvisor	C
★	C V	⋮	UnitedHealth Group	B
★	C V	⋮	VANGUARD S&P500	H
★	C V	⋮	VANGUARD S&P500	H
★	C V	⋮	Verizon Communicati...	A
★	C V	⋮	Visa Inc	B
★	C V	⋮	Vornado Realty Trust	C
★	C V	⋮	WESTERN DIGITAL ...	C
★	C V	⋮	Wal-Mart Stores	A
★	C V	⋮	Walgreens Boots Allia...	B
★	C V	⋮	Waste Management Inc	A
★	C V	⋮	Wells Fargo	C

If you were looking for what shares to buy, here's a nice job. Search in Google, you will find a lot of information. Go to official organizations of the stock exchange or the companies themselves.

Neither this list nor this book is a purchase recommendation, I only invite you to look for information about each of these companies and apply the analyses I mention in book one of this series because it works for me.

The technical analysis will tell you if it is time to buy, the fundamental analysis if it is a worthwhile company.

If it is on the list of favorites, it is most likely, in my opinion, a very interesting company. Although in which is not the best moment to invest or that, simply, does not fit with my strategy and I have better options (at this precise moment, in the future we will have to revise).

Remember, when doing your own stock research, use the English words to find the reports and investor information (use a translator or dictionary if necessary).

Update: The J. Biden Era and the Pfizer Vaccine

The stock market is going so well, it's worth an upgrade. On November 9 (Monday), with the announcement that the efficacy of the new Pfizer vaccine is 90% (and not 60%, as expected), the bags have shot up.

Aurora Cannabis has grown the most, and I've reaped benefits: I've sold some of my shares, for more than twice what they cost me, and I hope to keep selling as it continues to rise.

Also, in addition to renewables, there has been a great growth in confidence in tourism. In my Spanish portfolio I have closed positions in Melia Hotels, and in the American portfolio I hope to close positions in Carnival Corp. very soon.

Many stocks remain underpriced, affected by the poor outlook associated with the pandemic. But the solutions are also getting closer. Take advantage to enter before it is too late, if it is not already (it depends on what action, but there is still margin in many: airlines, tourism, renewable, real estate ...).

The result of the positive elections is very favorable for the markets, and invites us to think that growth has only just begun, that a very prosperous stage awaits us.

The combination of a Democratic president with a majority Republican parliament will not allow for major changes that could scare the markets, such as the return of corporate taxes that Trump eliminated.

There is a clear opportunity to invest in gold, which just today, Monday November 9, has fallen in price. I do it through the multinational mining company Barrick Gold, which has fallen by 10 %, the same as Pfizer. I thought about increasing my position (buying more shares of Barick Gold) since it is trading at a very good price, and when confidence in the rest of the economy falls, its value will rise again. The only thing that has stopped me is that it distributes dividend, but it doesn't allow the form with which the double imposition is reduced, for what it would have to pay the maximum of taxes, so much in EE. My interest is more like a growth stock, although I do not despise the dividend, the tax burden reduces it and is no longer too high.

In short, when the stock market rises it is not a good time to buy, but if you want to start positions do not postpone it indefinitely. Don't invest all your money at once, that way, if prices go down, you buy more and end up buying for a lower average price.

Right now I have automatic orders for the sale of several stocks that may reach their historical maximum soon. I prefer to get away with profit, actually, in the long run, I don't have faith in some of the companies I hold positions in. For example, American Express is making a lot of money, but if you look at countries in Asia, and even cities on other continents, the cards are already becoming obsolete. More and more payments are being made from cell phones.

Starbucks and Coca-Cola seem like excellent companies to me, but I also think they can hit the roof. And, if they do, I prefer to pull back, rather than watch it fluctuate. That's the way it is with me in general, I think historical highs are a good time to pull back, it's very likely to be the precedent of a correction (fall).

After all, the most profitable investment is not the stock market, it is business. The stock market is a perfect opportunity to put money to work that you don't need, and the coronavirus pandemic is the ideal time to do so, but it carries great risks: you don't control business.

For all this, if you want to take advantage of the wave of growth, go ahead. But remember that everything has its end. I will leave a part of my portfolio unsold in dividends, which I could keep for a lifetime, but with shares that I like very much or that are not yet at a price that can sell them and earn important sums (with respect to the prices for which I bought them).

Recommended books

https://www.amazon.com/Amazon-defense-Response-manifesto-against-ebook/dp/B08TV9YVQ6/ref=sr_1_14?dchild=1&qid=1615462771&refinements=p_27%3AAntonio+Robinhood&s=digital-text&sr=1-14&text=Antonio+Robinhood

https://www.amazon.com/Investing-market-beginners-experts-Internet-ebook/dp/B08TVKHZHX/ref=sr_1_11?dchild=1&qid=1615462771&refinements=p_27%3AAntonio+Robinhood&s=digital-text&sr=1-11&text=Antonio+Robinhood

INVEST IN THE STOCK MARKET 2020-2021

STRATEGY FOR MAKING MONEY FROM THE CORONAVIRUS PANDEMIC

ANTONIO ROBINHOOD

C. y C. EDICIONES

https://www.amazon.com/Invest-stock-market-2020-Coronavirus-ebook/dp/B08P21ZG14/ref=sr_1_16?dchild=1&qid=1615462771&refinements=p_27%3AAntonio+Robinhood&s=digital-text&sr=1-16&text=Antonio+Robinhood

https://www.amazon.com/Investing-Spanish-stock-market-2020-ebook/dp/B08P53Z7RN/ref=sr_1_12?dchild=1&qid=1615462771&refinements=p_27%3AAntonio+Robinhood&s=digital-text&sr=1-12&text=Antonio+Robinhood

https://www.amazon.com/gp/product/B08Y94LS8C?pf_rd_r=0WGAYAHW5EKAXKCS3T8X&pf_rd_p=5ae2c7f8-e0c6-4f35-9071-dc3240e894a8&pd_rd_r=aae095aa-8d9a-4bbb-a949-3c7554516494&pd_rd_w=LjRlY&pd_rd_wg=ooIky&ref_=pd_gw_unk

https://www.amazon.com/Investing-dividends-investing-achieving-financial-ebook/dp/B08Y837DL6/ref=sr_1_3?dchild=1&qid=1615462771&refinements=p_27%3AAntonio+Robinhood&s=digital-text&sr=1-3&text=Antonio+Robinhood

Translation from Spanish to English: Liliana Bogarín Cáceres.

www.ingramcontent.com/pod-product-compliance
Lightning Source LLC
Chambersburg PA
CBHW072237230526
45466CB00024B/2088